EXAMINATION OF CONSCIENCE

Based on the Ten Commandments

CHARLES MICHAEL

GIFTED BOOKS AND MEDIA

Copyright

Compiled by Charles Michael

Printed in the United States of America

Published in January 2020

Paperback ISBN: 978-1-947343-06-1

Published by Jayclad Publishing LLC
www.giftedbookstore.com

Table of Contents

Introduction

There are rules everywhere we go. Every institution has its rules. Every country, state, county, and town has its own set of rules and regulations for the good of its citizens. There are rules in each home. We tell our children what to do and what not to do. As a parent, I see that these rules are in the best interest of my children, although they may not understand or grasp them—the same works with God. Our heavenly Father has given us rules and regulations for our good while we are here in this life.

The law or the Ten Commandments, as it is commonly known, was given by God to Moses on Mount Sinai. The Greek word for the Ten Commandments is decalogue. The law of God holds an important place in the Jewish faith and most Christian denominations. The law was intended to be written not on stone alone but in every human heart. All the spiritual laws and sins are contained within the Ten Commandments. Every kind of sin that humankind has ever committed or will commit is stated within one of these commandments. The Ten Commandments is the best tool to examine our conscience, and it is the widely used tool in the Church to prepare for confession.

This book has a detailed examination based on the Ten Commandments, which will help us repent for our sins and prepare for a sincere and in-depth confession.

Charles Michael

Do's and Don't's of Confession

- Do not justify your sins
- Do not blame people or the circumstances for your sin
- Do not confess without repentance or preparation
- Do not be too detailed about sin
- Do not leave out any sin
- Do not postpone your confession
- Confess your sins regularly, if possible weekly
- Do not be picky about confessing to a priest. Go to any available priest
- Do not receive communion in a state of mortal sin. Confess your mortal sins before receiving communion
- Be sure to get rid of everything (people, substance) that tempts or leads you to sin
- Confess only your sins, not your problems
- Do not confess the sins of others
- Be mindful of the priest's time and others in line
- If in doubt about the seriousness of a sin, confess to the priest
- Do not be ashamed to confess any sin

- Do not hide your sins
- Do not lie in the confessional
- Do not make a false and insincere confession
- Do not confess a sin if it was already confessed and not committed
- Confessing venial sins helps us to be more sensitive to God and more faithful in our love to Him
- It is an excellent practice to write down the sins and take it to confession
- For a sin to be mortal, three conditions must be met: Mortal sins are sins whose object is grave matter and which is also committed with full knowledge and free will (full consent)
- Make reparation and restitution where and when necessary
- Forgive everyone unconditionally so that God may also forgive you
- Pray to the Holy Spirit to show you all hidden sins and to be filled with a heart of repentance
- Do not fail to do the penance given by the priest
- Be thankful for God's forgiveness

Note to the Reader

This book is a tool to examine one's conscience in order to prepare for a good confession. Not everything mentioned in this book is to be taken as a mortal sin or even requires confession. This book is a tool that will help us to identify areas that prevent us from going closer to God and help us become holier.

The Ten Commandments

List of the Ten Commandments

- I am the Lord your God, who brought you out of the land of Egypt, out of the house of slavery. You shall have no other gods before me
- You shall not make wrongful use of the name of the Lord your God
- Observe the sabbath day and keep it holy, as the Lord your God commanded you
- Honor your father and your mother
- You shall not kill
- You shall not commit adultery
- You shall not steal
- You shall not bear false witness against your neighbor
- You shall not covet your neighbor's wife
- You shall not covet your neighbor's goods

Where in the Bible, Do We Find the Commandments?

The Ten Commandments are listed in two places in the Old Testament and multiple places in the New Testament in parts. It is listed in Exodus, chapter 20, and Deuteronomy, chapter 5.

The First Commandment

I am the LORD your God, who brought you out of the land of Egypt, out of the house of bondage. You shall have no other gods before me.

Knowledge of God

- Do I seek and thirst to know God in prayer? How much quality time do I spend each day in worship, seeking and thirsting to know God?
- Do I study the Word of God every day?
- Do I meditatively reflect on sacred Scriptures every day?
- Am I regular to the sacraments? (Daily Eucharist if possible, Weekly confession, weekly fasting if healthy)
- If I cannot go for weekday Mass, do I at least meditate on the Mass readings of the day?
- Do I make time to read good Christian literature and works of saints to grow in the knowledge of God?
- Do I spend at least an hour a week in prayer before the blessed sacrament (Eucharistic Adoration)?
- Do I show interest in Godly and spiritual activities? (Lack of interest stems from a lack of love)

Love for God

- Do I have a fixed time for personal prayer every day?
- Do I look forward to my time with God (prayer time)?
- Are God and prayer the first things that come to my mind when I wake up each morning?
- Do I make it a point not to miss my personal prayer, no matter how busy or tired I am?
- Do I try to please God by finding out and doing what he expects of me?
- Do I try to know and learn God's laws and obey them?
- Do I hate and avoid doing what God hates?
- Am I able to see the hindrances and obstacles to my spiritual life and make the necessary sacrifices to be with God?
- Do I willfully make sacrifices to fulfill my relationship with God?
- Does my prayer time always gets compromised because of work, rest, and family commitments?
- Do I find it hard to come out of my comfort zone and make willful sacrifices for God?
- Do I talk to God outside of my prayer time?
- Do I think about God outside of Church?
- How often do I remember God outside of Church and prayer time?

- Do I feel bored or show a lack of interest at the very mention of prayer and Bible reading?
- Do I feel sleepy or tired as soon as I start praying or reading the Bible?
- Do I get distracted in my mind (thoughts) while praying or reading scripture?
- Have I harbored any hatred for God?

Worship of God

- Is my prayer God-centered or self-centered?
- Is my relationship with God restricted to receiving blessings and getting my prayers answered?
- Am I able to freely worship God without any demands?
- Am I holding on to something in place of God?
- Is there anything in my life that I value more than God?
- Am I giving God's place in my heart to a human being?
- Do I maintain reverence and proper posture when I pray?
- Have I associated myself or joined any group whose leader claims to be an incarnation of God?
- Did I leave my Catholic faith at any time?
- Did I worship any gods or goddesses of other religions?
- Do I give more importance to work and money than God?

- Am I in possession of any idols to whom I offer worship and honor?
- Did I worship, fear, or pay honor to any celestial body?
- Have I ever worshipped or feared nature?
- Have I worshipped the dead or had an unhealthy relationship with the deceased?
- Did I participate in any worship service of other religions or Christian denominations?
- Have I ever worshipped any animal or object?
- Do I celebrate or observe feasts and festivals of other religions?
- Do I revere any celebrity above the Almighty God, or do I have unhealthy respect or affiliation with a celebrity (Idolizing celebrities)?

Serve God

- Have I discovered my ministry of service for the Lord?
- Am I actively desiring and praying for a ministry?
- Do I make use of my natural talents, gifts, and abilities for the kingdom of God?
- Am I giving freely as I have received freely?
- In my service for the Lord, am I selfish and self-seeking?
- Do I have a deep thirst for the conversion of souls?
- Do I pray for others?

- Do I help others to find Christ?

Praise

- Do I praise God always and in all circumstances?
- Do I get tired or weary of praising God?
- Am I ashamed of praising God in front of others?
- Do I actively and whole-heartedly take part in singing during Mass?
- Do I sing praises to God at home?
- Have I judged anyone for praising aloud?
- Have I judged anyone for lifting their hands during prayer?
- Have I judged anyone for being loud and expressive during praise and worship in church?

Thanksgiving

- Do I thank God every day for all the material blessings?
- Do I thank God every day for all the people in my life, beginning with my parents, who brought me into this world?
- Do I thank God for all the opportunities and favors in life?
- Do I constantly complain to God about everything?
- Do I have the attitude of always focusing on the shortages in life?
- Do I thank God for the weaknesses and failures in life?

- Am I still thankful when nothing is going right in my life?
- Do I acknowledge everything as a gift from God?
- Am I a vocally complaining and a negative person?
- Am I able to thank God for all the people who hurt and wounded me?
- Am I able to thank God for all the missed opportunities in life?
- Am I forgetful of the many blessings that God has showered on me?

Prayer

- Do I pray every day?
- Do I pray solely for material needs?
- Do I long and pray for spiritual blessings?
- Have I surrendered everything in prayer?
- Do I have a desire to pray always?
- Do I pray for others?
- Do I miss or skip prayer because of the busyness and overload of work?
- Have I missed prayer because of tiredness and laziness?
- Do I enjoy my time with God?
- Am I always told or forced to pray by my family members?
- Am I distracted while praying?

- Do I see prayer as boring and mundane?
- Do I pray and seek God with all my heart?
- Did I give up on prayer because I did not see results?
- Do I pray about all things and always?
- Do I actively take part in my family prayer?
- Do I have a set time each day for personal prayer?
- Do I begin and end each day with prayer?
- Do I pray and call on God in times of trials and temptations?

Will of God

- Am I ambitious about worldly titles and rewards?
- Is my ambition in line with God's will?
- Do I seek the will of God in what I pray for?
- Am I reckless or rash in my decision making?
- Do I act without thinking, reasoning, or contemplating?
- Do I instinctively or impulsively make decisions without calculating the consequences?
- Do I wait on God to know his will in all matters?

Word of God (Bible)

- Do I read the Word of God every day?

- Do I prayerfully meditate on the Word every day?
- Do I write down what God is speaking to me each day through his word?
- Have I ever spoken against the Bible?
- Have I ever had doubts about the Bible being the Word of God?
- Do I share the Word with all family and friends, in person or through media?
- Do I defend and uphold the Word of God?
- Do I encourage people to read the Word of God?
- Did I treat the Bible with disrespect or contempt?

Holy Spirit

- Am I aware of the presence of the Holy Spirit in me?
- Do I thirst and long for God's Spirit in me?
- Do I actively pray for the gifts and charisms of the Holy Spirit?
- Do I take the help of the Holy Spirit during prayer and in times of temptation, dangers, trials, and decision making?
- Am I open to the gifts and charisms of the Holy Spirit?
- Have I judged people or ministries who use the gifts and charisms?
- Have I used the charisms for my own glory?

- Do I actively seek the fruits of the Holy Spirit and grow in them?
- Do I confess the negative fruits that are in me?
- Do I seek and pray for the fruits of the Holy Spirit that I lack?
- Do I see a priest or preacher as an idol?
- Do I give importance or value to a priest or lay people based on their charisms?
- Am I always trying to be friendly or contact people with specific charisms?
- Do I seek the help of people with charisms without having a relationship with God?
- Do I seek attention or glory while the charisms are manifested through me?
- Do I draw people to myself when I use the charisms and manifestations of the Holy Spirit?
- Have I sought any monetary gain or favors for the use of charisms?
- Do I, in any way, use the gifts and charisms for my personal monetary gain?
- Am I leading a life with holiness and love as the primary mission?
- Do I actively use the gifts/ charisms for the building up of the Church?
- Did I neglect to repent and confess my personal sins when the Holy Spirit convicted me?

- Did I grieve the Holy Spirit with my thoughts, words, and actions?

Faith

- Do I fear Satan and evil spirits?
- Do I fear sickness and death?
- Do I have any phobias?
- Do I worry about my life and future?
- Do I worry about my kids and their future?
- Do I worry about my finances and health?
- Do I have any insecurities, or am I too anxious about life?
- Have I doubted the existence of God?
- Have I doubted the real presence of Jesus in the Eucharist?
- Have I doubted that the Bible is the Word of God?
- Have I doubted the healing and saving power of God?
- Have I doubted any of the Church's teachings?
- Have I doubted the unconditional love of God for me?
- Have I doubted the love of God in times of suffering?
- Have I ever been Influenced by atheistic philosophers and their thinking?
- Do I presume in my own capacity to attain holiness and eternal life?

- Do I take the forgiveness of God for granted and keep adding sin to sin?
- Do I give in to despair when things do not go according to my wishes and plans?
- Have I ever denied the existence of God (apostasy)?
- Do I have a legalistic mindset or way of thinking?
- Did I ever doubt the oneness of the Father, the Son, and the Holy Spirit (Holy Trinity)?

Church

- Have I rebelled against the Holy Father or the Church in thoughts, words, and actions?
- Do I deliberately not adhere to the truth about God revealed by the Church?
- Do I go for my weekly confession?
- Do I examine my conscience and repent before going to confession?
- Did I hide any sin in confession?
- Do I set the example for all my family members in leading a sacramental life?
- Do I receive the sacraments with due respect and reverence?
- Did I ever leave the Church?
- Do I pick and choose the Church teachings that I want to believe?

- Do I leave out the Church teachings that I do not understand?
- Do I leave out teachings/rules that are hard for me to follow?
- Am I faithful to the Holy Father and my parish priest?
- Do I see the church and its laws as outdated and irrelevant to my way of thinking?
- Do I spend time reading the catechism and other church documents and grow in the knowledge of the Church?
- Have I spoken against the Church?
- Do I defend and uphold the teachings of the Church sincerely?
- Do I engage in any worldly conversation in church with other believers?
- Do I switch off all electronic gadgets that cause a distraction to myself and others?
- Am I adequately clothed and not tempting others with my attire?
- Do I genuflect when I enter and exit the sanctuary?
- Am I in a state of prayer, and is my mind entirely paying attention to what is happening in church without any distraction?
- Do I carry to church any unholy substance with me such as cigarettes, tobacco, drugs, or any secular literature?
- Do I observe Lent and Advent according to the requirements of the Church?
- Do I pray the Divine Mercy prayer at 3 o'clock every day (If time permits)?

- Am I obedient to the Church concerning fasting?
- Am I obedient to the Church concerning abstinence?
- Do I recite the way of the cross either individually or in a community (family or church) during Lent?
- Have I ever spoken against the Catholic tradition of using consecrated things?
- Am I a Catholic with all different kinds of scapulars and rosaries but with no prayer life?
- Do I regularly pray and intercede for my parish and parish priest?
- Do I sincerely pray for the Holy Father and all the religious?
- Have I spoken against a priest or religious?
- Have I judged a priest or a religious person?
- Have I mocked/ teased/ made fun of a religious person?
- Do I support religious people in their missions?
- Have I gossiped or spread rumors about a religious person?
- Do I envy the lifestyle of a religious person?
- Have I made unreasonable demands for receiving sacraments?
- Do I have any unforgiveness or bitterness toward the clergy?
- Is my relationship with my parish solely to attend the Sunday Mass?
- Have I put my God-given talents and gifts for the service of my parish and the whole Church?

- Do I financially support my parish and the evangelization efforts of the universal Church?
- Do I give my time for my parish and its missions?
- Do I participate and stay involved in any prayer group within my parish?
- Do I spend time adoring Jesus in the blessed sacrament if it is exposed in the parish?
- Have I lied to a priest in the confessional?
- Did I fail ever to do the penance advised by the priest in the confessional?
- Did I confess without trying to give up sin?
- Did I confess without repenting and feeling sorry for my sins?
- Did I confess without first getting rid of the object of sin?
- Have I committed the sin of simony (Simony is the act of selling church offices and roles or sacred things.)?
- Have I supported or been part of any schismatic group?
- Do I treat all things that are consecrated to God (such as relics, sacramentals) with respect and care?
- Have I lied to the church concerning my finances in order not to pay my tithes?
- Did I attend non-Catholic prayer meetings or worship thereby putting my Catholic faith in danger?
- Do I listen to non-Catholic talks and preachings thereby putting my Catholic faith in danger?
- Have I shown unbelief in any of the teachings of the Church?

- Do I use God's house (church) for anything other than worship and spiritual matters?
- Do I deliberately not go to confession because I want to continue in sin?
- Do I regularly examine my conscience?
- Did I deliberately overhear anybody's confession while waiting in line?

Mother Mary

- Do I honor the Blessed Mother as my own mother?
- Have I spoken anything against the blessed mother?
- Is my Marian devotion leading me closer to Jesus?
- Have I made mother Mary my sole mediator or an object of worship, thereby denying the power of Jesus and his work on the cross?
- Do I live by the messages of our lady given at various apparitions all over the world?
- Do I imitate Mary in virtues of humility, simplicity, obedience, and surrender?
- Have I judged anyone because of their Marian devotion?
- Do I always defend Mary's name and honor?
- Do I pray the Rosary everyday?

Saints

- Do I treat the saints, who are the members of the household of God, with honor and dignity?
- Have I spoken against the Catholic faith of honoring the saints?
- Have I judged the saintly devotion of other Christians?
- Have I at any time given more value and importance to saints than to God?
- Have I ever spoken against the Catholic teaching on the intercession of saints?

Angels

- Have I ever treated heavenly beings equal to God?
- Have I placed my trust in any of the heavenly beings without first loving God?
- Have I given more time and importance to any heavenly being other than God?

Superstition

- Do I believe in superstition?
- Do I see or treat numbers as lucky or unlucky?
- Do I see any colors to be either lucky or unlucky?
- Do I treat any days or dates to be auspicious or inauspicious?

- Do I believe in making wishes on events?
- Do I possess any objects that claim to bring me luck?
- Do I celebrate any non-Christian festivals (occult, festivals of other religions) or feasts?
- Did I put my trust in any man-made object or things from the natural world to protect me or bring good luck?
- Do I follow any non-Christian traditions that goes against my faith?

Occult

- Do I have an unhealthy attachment with any of my deceased family members?
- Have I communicated or contacted any dead person directly or with the help of a medium?
- Do I practice any pagan or occult exercise or workout methods such as yoga?
- Do I use any non-Christian meditation technique to relax my mind and body?
- Have I worn any non-Christian jewelry, pendants, good-luck charms, or Talisman? Do I keep any non-Christian artifact in my house for good luck, healing, protection, or blessing?
- Have I used any occult means such as Reiki, for the healing of sicknesses?
- Have I resorted to any occult rituals to come out of debt or financial problems?

- Did I seek any supernatural powers or blessings through the occult?
- Have I used any occult powers to control, manipulate, or harm people?
- Did I cast any spell on people?
- Have I used any occult powers to know my future or any information?
- Am I in possession of any occult literature or media?
- Do I celebrate any pagan festivals?
- Did I participate in any Satanic ritual or worship?
- Did I have any tie or membership with any Satanic group or cult?
- Do I watch or listen to any ungodly shows, movies, or music?
- Did I practice any sorcery or black magic?
- Did I use astrology as a means to know my past, present, or future?
- Did I take the help of fortune tellers to know future events?
- Did I consult any seances or mediums?
- Did I seek to know about the future through horoscopes, numerology, and palmistry?
- Have I used birth charts or depended on zodiac signs for luck and information about my life and the future?
- Have I used occult practices such as witchcraft, Ouija boards, tarot cards, and hypnotism?

- Have I been part of any secret society such as the freemasons?
- Have I been involved with the New Age Movement, atheism, agnosticism, or eastern philosophies?
- Do I have a liking for horror movies, or have I watched any since my last confession?

The Second Commandment

You shall not take the name of the Lord your God in vain

Use of God's Name

- Do I invoke the name of the Trinity each morning when I wake up?
- Do I invoke and begin all things in the name of the Trinity?
- Do I invoke the Trinity each time I drive or begin a meal?
- Do I invoke the Trinity each night before going to bed?
- Do I call on the name of God when I am tempted or when I face trials?

Misuse of God's Name

- Have I ever made fun of God?
- Have I ever made fun of other Christians, especially their faith and style of worship?
- Have I ever made fun of the manifestations of the charisms of the Holy Spirit in the Church or other Christians?

- Have I ever made fun of people who approached me with the message about Jesus?
- Do I mock or make fun of my family members or others for their excessive faith?
- Do I get angry and curse when unpleasant things happen to me?
- Am I angry at God for my sufferings?
- Am I angry at God for my sickness or the sicknesses of my family members?
- Do I curse or use bad language which involves the name of God?
- Do I watch or listen to any media that disrespectfully speak about God?
- Have I used God's name in a profane or unholy way?
- Have I joked about God?
- Have I used God's name irreverently or casually?
- Did I ever blame God for my sufferings or weaknesses?
- Do I use the name of God in my conversations in an offensive way?
- Have I watched any movie or TV show that talks about God in an offensive way?
- Have I listened to songs, talk shows, stand-up comedy shows that refer to God in an offensive way?
- Have I made any promises to God and not tried to keep them?
- Did I swear using God's name?

- Did I blaspheme or speak against God?
- Have I had negative thoughts about God?
- Have I ever spoken negatively about God, especially his love and mercy?
- Have I ever seen God as partial or biased?
- Do I see God as cruel?
- Did I ever blame God for my failures?

Satan

- Have I ever denied the existence of Satan?
- Do I blame Satan for all evil, sickness, and suffering in my life?
- Am I always talking about Satan?
- Do I fear Satan (Satanophobia)?
- Do I blame Satan for all temptations and sin?

Sacred Scripture

- Do I read the Word of God in its entirety?
- Do I misquote and tweak scripture to live by my own beliefs and standards?
- Have I misled other people due to my limited understanding of God?
- Do I read the Word of God enthusiastically (with devotion)?

Evangelization

- Did I ever incite any violence in the name of religion?
- Have I been part of any religious hate group or any religious supremacy groups?
- Do I look at people of other faiths with ridicule and condemnation?
- Do I have hatred and contempt for people of other faiths?
- Am I embarrassed or ashamed to pray in public?
- Am I open about my Christian faith and beliefs?
- Have I at any time failed to testify my faith in Jesus?
- Can people see Jesus and his qualities in me?
- Have I made my Catholic faith attractive to others?

Vows and Promises

- Do I fulfill all the promises that I make to God?
- Do I abide by the promises I make to others, in the name of God?
- Do I keep the promises I make to God when I repent and confess my sins?
- Have I lied in a court under oath (perjury)?
- Did I make any false claims or lie to immigration officials or any authority?

- Am I honest when I speak about myself?
- Have I lied about my qualification or experience when seeking a job?

The Third Commandment

Remember the sabbath day, to keep it holy

Importance of The Lord's Day

- Do I treat Sunday as a "work from home" day?
- Do I occupy myself with worldly activities on the Lord's day?
- Do I stay awake Saturday nights and sleep through Sunday?
- Do I occupy myself with work that takes me away from my family and church?
- Do I spend the Lord's day in idleness?

Employers and Businesspeople

- Do I force or make it mandatory for my employees to work on Sundays?
- Do I send employees with work to be completed on Sundays?
- Do I keep my non-essential business open on Sundays?

Holy Mass

- Did I miss Mass on Sunday since my last confession?
- Do I attend Mass daily if time permits?
- Have I ever attended Mass without fasting for an hour (If health permits)?
- Have I attended Mass in a drunken state or under the influence of drugs?
- Do I go to Mass willfully and joyfully?
- Do I meditate on the day's readings before or after Mass?
- Do I deliberately/ habitually come to Mass late and leave early?
- Do I fail or forget to attend Mass on holy days of obligation?
- Do I fail to show reverence to God by not genuflecting, standing, and kneeling during Mass (if healthy)?
- Did I dress indecently and immodestly for Mass?
- Did I doubt in the real presence of Jesus in the Eucharist?
- Do I pray for people who have asked for my intercession (during Mass)?
- Do I unconditionally forgive and love my enemies and pray for them during Mass?
- Am I able to concentrate on the Mass proceedings without any distractions?
- Do I listen attentively to the Mass readings, sermon, and prayers, or do I easily get distracted?

- Do I actively take part in the Mass prayers and worship by listening and responding?
- Do I keep the conversation with other believers to the minimum and not talk about worldly things?
- Do I switch off all my gadgets or put them on silent mode before Mass begins?
- Do I attend Mass with all my family members?
- Have I received communion in a state of mortal sin?
- Do I distract others during Mass?
- Did I ever show reluctance or lack of interest in partaking of the Holy Communion?
- Have I ever stolen the Holy Communion (host) or taken it home (sacrilege)?

The Fourth Commandment

Honor your father and your mother, so that your days may be long in the land that the Lord your God is giving you.

Children (Under 18) Living with Their Parents

- Do I always have to be rewarded for doing anything?
- Have I ever disobeyed my parents or elders?
- Have I ever ignored the commands or directions of my parents?
- Do I have to be repeatedly reminded or told to do things that are expected of me?
- Do I manipulate my parents with my tantrums?
- Do I deliberately do or say things that will cause my parents to lose their temper?
- Have I ever grieved my parents?
- Do I complain about education and homework?
- Do I cooperate when my parents ask me to pray?

- Do I talk back to my parents, teachers, or elders?
- Have I brought dishonor to my parents through my actions in school or outside of home?
- Have I shown disrespect to elders?
- Am I kind and gentle with other children?
- Do I fail or forget to pray for my parents?
- Have I been unkind or rude to others?
- Do I have to be continuously told to do my daily chores and duties?
- Do I feel unloved at home?
- Do I see discipline as something that goes against my freedom?
- Have I had thoughts of leaving home or running away?
- Do I see my parents as my enemies?
- Do I rebel against elders in the family?
- Do I watch too much television or the internet that hinders my education?
- Do I put my heart in education and learning, or do I see it as a burden?
- Am I prompt in doing all my schoolwork on time?
- Do I deliberately make excuses to stay away from school and learning?
- Do I show a lack of interest in learning about God?

- Do I fail to prepare well for tests and exams?
- Do I fail to seek God's help every day for my education?
- Am I addicted to toys, video games, and gadgets?
- Do I spend too much time talking/ chatting with my friends?
- Do I give more importance to games, sports, and entertainment than education?
- Do I share everything with my parents?
- Do I make my parents part of everything in my life?
- Am I hiding any grave sin/ habit from my parents?
- Do I watch anything on television or the internet without my parent's knowledge and consent?
- Do my parents know all my friends?
- Did I talk to any adult without my parent's knowledge either on the internet or in person?
- Is there any incident in my life (e.g., sexual abuse) that I am hiding from my parents?
- Do I resist to help my parents with household chores?
- Do I always have to be told to clean my room?
- Does somebody have to always clean up after me?
- Do I have to be told repeatedly to do things around the house?
- Do I share everything with God?
- Have I lied to my parents about anything?

- Do I pray every day for my parents and siblings?
- Do I begin everything with a prayer?
- Do I pray for wisdom in studies/academics?
- Do I pray for protection every day?
- Do I, in faith, lift the needs of the family in prayer?
- Do I see my sibling as a competitor and a rival?
- Do I get these thoughts that my parents love my sibling more than they like me?
- Do I feel that my parents give more time and attention to my siblings than to me?
- Do I act unkindly toward my siblings and fail to love them?
- Do I have trouble sharing things with my siblings?
- Do I fail to pray for my sibling?
- Have I been moody and rebellious about prayer and going to Mass on Sunday?
- Have I gotten angry at anybody, or have I hit anyone?
- Have I treated other children with respect, or have I made fun of them and called them names?

Adult's Relationship with Parents

- Do I forget to remember my parents every day in prayer?
- Do I look at my parents with gratitude?

- Have I ever blamed my parents for giving birth to me?
- Have I ever blamed my parents for the hardships in life?
- Have I ever blamed my parents for the missed opportunities in life?
- Have I ever blamed my parents for the decisions they took in my life?
- Do I have any unforgiveness, resentment, or hatred toward my parents?
- Did I ever verbally abuse my parents?
- Did I ever physically abuse my parents?
- Did I insult my parents in front of others?
- Did I yell or raise my voice against my parents?
- Have I ever cursed my parents?
- Do I care for my aged and weak parents without complaining?
- Do I take them for their hospital visits if there is a need?
- Do I attend to their basic needs if they are disabled and sick?
- Do I see my weak parents as a burden?
- Have I ever wished that they should die?
- Do I stay in touch with my elderly parents?
- Do I inquire, or am I aware of their present health condition and wellbeing?
- Do I visit them often if they are not living with me?

- Am I aware of the financial needs of my aged parents and help them if they are in need?
- Am I willing to accommodate them if they have no place to go?
- Do I care for and visit my sick and disabled parents?
- Have I ever kicked out my parents from home?

Parents with Children (Under 18)

- Have I loved and accepted my child from the moment of its conception?
- Did I expectantly look forward to the birth of my child?
- Did I, at any time, see my child as a burden?
- Was I at any time physically and deliberately unavailable for my children during their growing years?
- Did I express my love through touch and eye contact during the initial infancy/toddler years of my child?
- Do I spend enough time with my child?
- Have I at any time rejected my children due to some weakness or disability in them?
- Do I compare my child with other children?
- Did I ever physically, verbally, or sexually abuse my child?
- Do I have unjust and unrealistic demands and expectations from my children?

- Am I compassionate and considerate to my children in their weaknesses?
- Have I ever criticized, condemned, or ridiculed my child?
- Do I pray for my child?
- Do I correct my child often?
- Have I neglected correction at any time?
- Does my discipline come from a love for the child or out of my negative character or personality?
- Do I give excess love to my child without discipline?
- Do I let my child get away with unruly behavior?
- Do I sometimes find it too hard or tiring to discipline my child?
- Do I yield to my children's tantrums to quiet them?
- Do I spoil my children with too many toys?
- Do I let them have their way with television/ video games?
- Do I, as a parent, have a poor personal relationship with God?
- Do I see the area of faith as the sole responsibility of the Church and not my own?
- Do I introduce Bible stories and saints' lives to my children through books and movies?
- Do I read the Bible to my children and make them learn when they are ready?
- Do I take time to pray with my children?

- Do I talk to my children about God?
- Do I instruct my children about our Catholic faith?
- Do I take my children to Mass regularly?
- Do I take time and show interest in preparing my children for the Sacraments?
- Do I correct my child when he or she has trouble adjusting or interacting with people?
- Do I teach my child to respect all elders?
- Do I instruct my child about reaching out to others in their need?
- Do I teach my child to forgive and to love all?
- Do I lead my child in praying for others?
- Am I patient with my child?
- Do I teach good morals and godly values to my child?
- Do I stay involved with my child's academics?
- Do I take the time to tutor my child?
- Do I give responsibilities to my children and make them accountable?
- Do I feel used when I am asked to provide for my family?
- Do I feel like a servant at home?
- Do I take charge and responsibility for the financial needs of the family?

- Do I instruct my children, the importance of money management?
- Have I ever seen family life as a burden?
- Am I aware of the whereabouts of my children, where and with whom they are?
- Do I teach my child the importance of modesty in clothing?
- Have I given up my hobbies and interests in life that keep me away from my children and family?
- Do I habitually leave my child with others so that I can indulge in my hobbies and passions?
- Have I put my child in any danger?
- Do I sin in front of my children (smoke, drink, etc.)?
- Do I treat my spouse with respect and dignity, especially in front of my children?
- Am I a good model for my children?
- Do I preach anything to my children and not practice?
- Can my children see in me an active and strong parent?
- Are my weaknesses affecting my children?
- Do I value God and family more than anything else?

Parents of Adult Children

- Am I guiding my adult children in their decisions?
- Am I interfering in my children's marriage and life?

- Am I available for them when they need advice?
- Do I pray for my children and their families?

Marriage Partners

- Do I unconditionally love my spouse?
- Have I accepted all the imperfections and weaknesses of my spouse unconditionally?
- Are the weaknesses and imperfections in my spouse, causing a burden in loving my spouse?
- Have the physical and personality changes of my spouse over time hindered my love?
- Do I joyfully make sacrifices for my marriage and spouse?
- Has my selfishness and self- centeredness ever caused a rift in the marriage?
- Have I ever had thoughts of separating or divorcing my spouse?
- Have I ever been unjustly angry toward my spouse?
- Did I ever physically or verbally abuse my spouse?
- Do I complain about my spouse to other people?
- Do I put my self-interest above the interests of the family?
- Do I talk disrespectfully about my spouse?
- Have I gossiped about my spouse?
- Am I compassionate and merciful to my spouse?

- Am I forgiving?
- Do I give more importance to my children than my spouse?
- Do I ignore or neglect my spouse?
- Have I helped my spouse get closer to Jesus after marriage?
- Does my spouse see godly qualities in me?
- Have I made Jesus and the Catholic faith appealing to my spouse through my words and actions?
- Do I pray with my spouse?
- Do I treat my spouse as my slave?
- Am I withholding any of my spouse's fundamental rights?
- Have I or do I see marriage or family life as a prison?
- Do I give due respect to my spouse?
- Am I still living like a single person after marriage?
- Have I given up friendships, hobbies, passions that conflict with my marriage?
- Have I given up all friendships with the opposite sex (ex-girlfriends, etc.) after marriage?
- Am I faithful to my spouse when he or she is not around?
- Is my spouse the only person in my mind, or do I secretly think or fantasize about being with somebody else?
- Do I compare my spouse with others?
- Do I have any addictions that my spouse is not aware of?

- Do I share everything with my spouse?
- Am I able to communicate freely with my spouse?
- Am I always available for my spouse?
- Do I enjoy my spouse's company?
- Do I have friends that my spouse is not aware of?
- Do I value my work and carrier more than my marriage and family?
- Do I have any financial or business dealings without the knowledge of my spouse?
- Does my spouse have access to my phone and other gadgets?
- Do I have contacts with people of the opposite sex without the knowledge and consent of my spouse?
- Do I still entertain thoughts about my past romantic relationships?
- Am I in contact with my ex-girl/boyfriends?
- Am I in contact with people with whom I have had sexual relations?
- Have I lied or been deceitful to my spouse?
- Do I treat my spouse's relatives (in-laws) with love and respect?
- Do I support my spouse in his or her career choices and aspirations?
- Have I been envious or jealous about my spouse for any reason?

Authority of the Husband

- Do I, as a husband, use the God-given authority to lead my family in holiness and love?
- Have I ever abused the God-given authority?
- Do I fail to use my God-given authority?
- Do I lead my family in prayer every day?

Wives, Submit to your Husbands

- Do I resist to submit to my husband's authority?
- Have I ever rejected my husband's authority?
- Do I see myself superior to my husband?
- Do I do things or make decisions without my husband's knowledge or consent?
- Do I see and recognize my husband as the head of the family?
- Have I undermined the authority and dignity of my spouse through disrespect and rebelliousness?

Husbands, Love Your Wives

- Am I considerate and understanding toward my wife?
- Do I listen to my wife and take suggestions from her?
- Do I give time to my spouse and her needs?
- Am I patient with my wife?

- Have I honored my spouse with my total affection and exclusive love?
- Have I at any time physically abused my spouse?
- Have I caused tensions and fights with my wife and failed to pursue peace with her?

Family Responsibilities

- Do I spend a lot of time outside the home with friends or at the gym and not pay attention to the needs of the family?
- Am I a lazy person, not helping my spouse and children?
- Do I have passions and hobbies that conflict with my family time and responsibilities?
- Do I complain about my responsibilities at home?
- Do I financially support my family if there is a need?
- Is my unhealthy lifestyle causing undue burdens on my family members?

Togetherness

- Do I always make plans with my friends and absent myself from my family?
- Do I spend too much time on media and gadgets?
- Do we eat together as a family?
- Do I make myself available for the family prayer?
- Do I give more time and importance to my social media friends than my family?

Civic Responsibilities

- Do I obey all the laws of the land sincerely (as long as it does not conflict with God's law)?
- Do I follow all traffic rules?
- Do I obey the authority that God has put over me, namely at work, school, and church?
- Do I participate and vote in all elections for the candidates who stand for and uphold ethical Christian values?
- Do I follow the laws about cleanliness in public places?
- Do I exercise my rights in all civic matters?
- Am I a silent spectator when evil, lawlessness, and wickedness is increasing around me?
- Do I stand up and support those who do not have rights or whose rights are being taken away?
- Have I supported, endorsed, or voted for a politician whose positions are opposed to the teachings of Jesus and the Catholic Church?
- Do I actively pray for all leaders and all those whom God has put as authority over me?

People in Authority

- Have I, a man of authority, ever brought dishonor to the name of God?
- Have I, with my full conscience, represented the Christian faith in voicing my opinions?

- Do I sincerely work for the cause of the poor and the minority?
- Have I supported or endorsed any law that goes against Christian teaching?
- Am I a good Christian to all those who are under me?
- Did I ever hide my Christian faith or identity in front of others?
- Are my political and social opinions in line with my Christian teachings?

The Fifth Commandment

Thou shall not Kill

Pro-Life

- Have I committed abortion and not confessed the sin? (If the sin was confessed, parents should let go and not live in guilt, but believe that the child is with God)
- Have I been part of any pro-choice group such as planned parenthood, etc.?
- Have I advised or suggested anyone to get an abortion?
- Do I actively fight for the rights of the unborn?
- Have I performed an abortion or assisted in the procedure of abortion to anyone (*for medical professionals*)?
- Have I voted for or supported any pro-choice candidates to public office?
- Have I funded or contributed to any pro-choice organization or institution?
- Have I formally cooperated in an abortion?
- Do I judge people who have committed an abortion?

- Have I endorsed, supported, or sponsored any research that destroys human embryos?
- Did I prefer one gender over the other when desiring for a child?
- Did I abort a child because of some congenital disabilities in them?
- Did I abort a child because of gender?
- Have I involved in or supported human cloning?

Murder

- Have I intentionally and unjustly murdered anyone?
- Have I had murderous thoughts toward anyone?
- Have I encouraged anyone to commit murder?
- Have I killed anyone out of negligence?
- Do I possess any illegal weapons (guns, arms) that are dangerous to the lives of people who live with me?
- Do I watch or have an interest in movies and shows filled with violence?
- Have I supported any terrorist organization or hate group?
- Have I indirectly cooperated in a murder?
- Have I inflicted bodily harm on another person?
- Have I threatened another person with bodily harm?
- Have I refused assistance to a person in danger?

- Have I ever supported and encouraged capital punishment?
- Have I ever supported or encouraged euthanasia (mercy killing)?
- Have I supported any unjust war at any time?

Hatred, Discrimination, Favoritism, and Partiality

- Have I been partial to people with good looks?
- Have I been partial to the rich and influential?
- Have I ever, acting as a person of authority, been partial to my friends and family members?
- Have I received favors from people by misusing God-given qualities such as good looks?
- Have I discriminated against anybody based on their color, political affiliation, caste, race, religion, sexual orientation, etc.?
- Am I cruel to minorities or people who have immigrated from other countries or places?
- Have I entertained any thoughts of hatred, grudge, or revenge?
- Did I refuse forgiveness to anyone?
- Have I willfully engaged in unjust lawsuits?
- Have I committed the sin of bigotry (hatred for people of other races)
- Have I committed the sin of nepotism (favoring relatives or friends over deserving people)?

- Am I a member of any supremacy group?

Suicide

- Have I ever attempted to take my life?
- Have I had suicidal thoughts?
- Have I encouraged, suggested, or assisted anyone in committing suicide?
- Have I, by my words, actions, and behavior caused anyone to attempt suicide?

Respect for the Body

- Have I committed any acts of self-mutilation?
- Have I performed excessive body piercings (not including ears and nose for wearing jewelry)?
- Have I committed or considered the act of self-immolation (killing oneself for a social or political cause)?
- Did I destroy my body (the temple of the Holy Spirit) with excessive tattoos?
- Do I take good care of my body by giving it enough rest and eating healthy foods?
- Did I opt for any plastic surgery to enhance my looks and appearance?
- Did I undergo any unhealthy weight loss programs thereby harming my overall health and wellbeing?

- Do I use excessive makeup to enhance my looks and appearance?

Substance Addictions

- Do I smoke at home, thereby exposing my family members' health to various sicknesses?
- Do I sincerely pray and try to get freedom from smoking and alcohol?
- Do I educate myself about the harm and side effects of alcohol and tobacco?
- Do I have the habit of driving a vehicle or operating machinery after the consumption of alcohol?
- Have I consumed alcohol while being pregnant, thereby affecting the health of the unborn baby?
- Have I consumed alcohol and taken prescribed medication, thereby putting my life at risk?
- Have I misbehaved with others in a state of drunkenness?
- Do I make a sincere effort to flee from people or company/ friendships whose primary hobby is to drink and party?
- Have I violated somebody sexually, verbally, or physically after consuming alcohol?
- Did I ever commit any grave sin under the influence of alcohol?
- Did I ever promote, buy, or tempt underage people (minors) to smoke, drink, or consume drugs?

- Did I introduce alcohol or tobacco to others and cause them to sin?
- Do I browse/ text while driving?
- Has my media addiction affected the people who live with me?
- Has my media addiction affected my work at any time?
- Do I go through chronic impulses to look at the screen (signs of addiction)?
- Do I feel uneasy, agitated, and sad when I am away from my phone or if it is turned off or there is no signal or connectivity?
- Do I experience behavioral change when the phone is taken away from me?
- Do I put my health at risk by my addiction such as staying up late and browsing the internet for no valid reason?
- Am I addicted to, or do I use any banned substances classified as drugs?
- Am I addicted to any medication that is prescribed to me?
- Have I abused medicines at any time?
- Am I addicted to unhealthy junk food?
- Am I addicted to caffeinated drinks or soft drinks?

Destructive Habits

- Do I overspeed or drive negligently, thereby putting myself and others' lives at risk?

- Do I text or use my phone while driving?
- Am I involved in any game, sport, passion, or hobby that is life-threatening and dangerous?
- Do I obey my doctor to a reasonable level?
- Do I willfully destroy or bring harm to nature and the world around me?
- Do I promptly recycle products as per the law of the land?

Friendships and Bad Company

- Do I make a sincere effort to flee from friendships that lead me to sin?
- Am I a people-pleasing person, thereby compromising on my Christian values?
- Do I flee from immoral company?
- Have I supported or been part of another person's grave sin?
- Do I flee from friendships/ people who pose a threat to my Christian faith and morals?

Forgiveness

- Have I forgiven all my enemies?
- Have I forgiven all those who hurt and wounded me?
- Have I made peace with all?

The Sixth Commandment

You shall not commit adultery

Sexuality Within Marriage

- Have I deprived my spouse of the marital right, without just cause (conjugal rights)?
- Did I ever act in selfishness when it came to sexual relations with my spouse
- Did I ever see sex as a mere act of pleasure without an expression of love?
- Did I ever see my spouse as an object of sex or gratification?
- Am I yielding and considerate to my spouse in the area of sex?
- Do I cooperate when my spouse asks for sexual abstinence to pray?
- Do I publicly display sexual affection toward my spouse?
- Have I used or forced/ encouraged my spouse to use artificial methods of contraception?
- Did I indulge in any unhealthy fetishes?
- Have I refused sexual relations to my spouse out of laziness, revenge, manipulation, or anger?

- Have I used sexual relations solely for my own selfish pleasure?
- Have I been too demanding in my desire for sexual fulfillment?
- Have I been loving and affectionate in my sexual relations, or have I used sex in a way that would be demeaning or disrespectful to my spouse?
- Did I force any sexual practice on my spouse that he or she was not comfortable?
- Do I fantasize or imagine other people while having sex with my spouse?
- Have I committed the sin of onanism (intentional withdrawal or non-vaginal ejaculation)?
- Have I used any birth control pills to avoid pregnancy?
- Have I used any artificial family planning methods to avoid pregnancy?

Sex Outside of Marriage

- Have I knowingly associated with any married person of the opposite sex without any valid reason?
- Have I committed the sin of divorce or separated from my spouse (not applicable to victims of divorce)?
- Have I committed adultery?
- Have I committed fornication?
- Did I engage in any sexual activity with my fiance'/ fiancee'?

- Did I ever support or be a part of a polygamous union (married to more than one person at the same time)?
- Did I ever cohabit (man and woman living together before marriage)?
- Did I support or be part of a trial marriage?
- Did I support or be part of an open relationship?
- Did I support or be part of a swinging relationship (partner swapping)?
- Did I engage in sexual foreplay, which is reserved for marriage?
- Am I a promiscuous person (having or characterized by many transient sexual relationships)?

Sex as a Commodity

- Have I engaged in any phone sex?
- Do I spend time in chatrooms, apps, or social media engaging in profane conversations?
- Have I used any sex toys, foreplay toys, or adult magazines?
- Have I used sex-enhancing drugs?
- Have I viewed any webcam or live-sex videos?
- Have I been part of any webcam shows (sexual)?
- Have I used sex to earn money?
- Have I visited a prostitute or bought sex?

- Have I watched any porn or adult movie?
- Have I acted in any porn or adult movie?
- Have I sold or exchanged any adult movies or materials?
- Have I used my body as a bribe or to receive a favor?
- Have I used my body to gain power, influence, promotion, etc.?
- Do I read sexually explicit novels and stories, pornographic books and magazines?

Unnatural Sexual Practices

- Have I had sexual thoughts toward my family members other than my spouse?
- Did I ever commit the sin of incest (sex with family members other than my spouse)?
- Have I ever tempted any of my family members by my conversation or the way I dress or behave?
- Did I make any advances or force any of my family members (other than spouse) to sexual activities?
- Did I ever sexually abuse an animal?
- Did I ever have any unhealthy sexual relationships with animals (bestiality)?
- Did I commit the sin of masturbation?
- Do I have any unhealthy sexual fetishes?
- Have I committed the sin of transvestism or cross-dressing?

- Have I participated in any acts of public nudity?
- Have I engaged in any group sex activity?

Homosexuality

- Have I ever indulged in same-sex acts with anyone?
- Have I watched same-sex videos and media?
- Did I ever support the legalizing of the homosexual union?
- Have I or do I entertain homosexual thoughts or desires within me?
- Have I ever attended a same-sex marriage ceremony?
- Have I endorsed or supported same-sex marriage either online or in a conversation?
- Have I judged or discriminated people with homosexual tendencies?

Sexual Violence / Sex by Force

- Did I rape anyone?
- Did I sexually violate, abuse, or molest another person (groping)?
- Did I make any forceful sexual advances toward another person?
- Did I demand sexual favors for any reason?
- Have I committed the sin of pedophilia?

- Have I had sexual relations with a minor?
- Did I make any unwanted or unwelcomed sexual advances toward another?
- Have I watched child pornography?
- Have i transmitted or uploaded nude pictures of people (revenge porn) over the internet?

Luring Others to Sex / Sexually Immoral Person

- Did I touch others or let others touch me in an impure manner?
- Did I lure or tempt others to commit any sexual sin?
- Did I yield to another person's sexual advances?

The Seventh Commandment

Thou shall not steal

Stealing from God

Tithing

- Do I tithe regularly?
- Do I financially support my local parish?
- Have I denied anyone who sought help from me for doing God's work?
- Do I tithe cheerfully, or do I give under compulsion, or is it guilt-driven?
- Am I generous in giving?
- Do I give the best of everything or give leftovers for God's kingdom?

Stealing God's Money

- Have I ever stolen tithe money?
- Have I ever misused tithe money?

- Have I used tithe money for personal reasons?
- Do I pray for direction in using tithe money?

Stealing from Neighbor

- Have I ever shoplifted?
- Have I stolen anything from any institution that I am part of (Example: school, college, library, church, workplace, etc.)?
- Have I stolen money from my parents when living with them?
- Have I been involved in any theft or robbery?

Accidental Damage to Others' Property or Public Property

- Have I caused damage to another's property due to my negligence and have not taken responsibility for it?
- Have I tried to restore or make restitution for the damage caused by me?
- If the damage is not repairable or not restorable, do I at least pray for the victims?

Vandalism

- Have I vandalized any public or private property as an act of revenge?
- Have I vandalized others' property to make a statement or to express my views?

- Have I vandalized public or private property under the influence of alcohol or drugs?

Wages and Salary

- Have I, as an employer, unjustly withheld the wages of my employees?
- Do I pay my employees promptly?
- Do I pay what I have promised and agreed?
- Do I pay what everyone deserves?

Taxes, Bills, Debts, & Dues

- Do I sincerely try to come out of debt and pray about it?
- Have I identified the areas in my family that has led us to this situation (debt) and resolve not to repeat it?
- Do I promptly pay all taxes owed?
- Do I promptly pay all bills and dues?
- Did I fail to honor my part of a contract?

Collecting taxes & Charging Interest

- Am I compassionate to the one who owes me money?
- Am I considerate to people when I use my authority to collect any debt or interest?
- Have I given a reasonable time to all my debtors to return the money owed?

Bribe

- Did I ever accept a bribe for my services?
- Did I ever give a bribe for a service?
- Did I ever demand a bribe for a service?

Business Dealings

- Am I open and honest with all my business partners about the business activities and profits (and losses)?
- Do I provide quality products to my customers?
- Do I deliver the products in the quality that I advertised it?
- Do I make unmerited and false claims of the product or the services I provide?
- Am I prompt and timely in delivering my products and services?
- Did I overcharge for my services?

Extortion of Money

- Have I unjustly used force, blackmail, or threats to recover the money that people owe me?
- Do I give reasonable time to my debtors to pay back what they owe me?
- Am I patient, considerate, and compassionate to the one who owes me anything?
- Have I used illegal means to extort money?

Plagiarism

- Did I copy or use another person's literary work and claim it as my own?
- Did I copy or use another person's literary work without giving credit or compensation?

Piracy (Copyright Infringement)

- Have I stolen others' work and claimed it as my own?
- Have I used others' work without permission?
- Have I used others' work without crediting or compensating them?
- Have I patented something which was not my creation?
- Have I knowingly downloaded media from illegal websites?
- Have I knowingly uploaded or transmitted content over the internet without permission?
- Do I watch movies or shows from pirated or illegal websites?

Encroachment, Slavery, and Kidnapping

- Did I ever kidnap or hold a person captive for ransom?
- Did I assist in any kidnapping activity?
- Did I extract labor from a person against his will?
- Did I infringe on another person's property by legal or illegal means?
- Did I claim ownership of property that did not belong to me?

- Have I committed the sin of human trafficking?

Counterfeiting, Adulteration, and Forgery

- Did I ever buy (with knowledge) or sell counterfeit goods and services?
- Did I sell an adulterated product to customers?
- Did I forge any documents for personal gain?
- Have I cheated on tests, exams, sports, or games?

Partiality/ Favoritism

- Did I show partiality to anyone to receive a favor in return?
- Did I commit the sin of nepotism?

Fraud, Hacking, Identity Theft, and False Claims

- Have I made any false claims to receive coverage, money, or benefits?
- Have I stolen people's money through any Ponzi or investment schemes?
- Did I hack any network or computer system to steal data or spread a virus?
- Did I steal or misuse another person's identity?
- Do I mistreat people, or am I partial to people whom I like?
- Have I scammed or defrauded anyone?

Stealing / Wasting People's Time / Misuse of Time

- Do I waste my time at work?
- Have I misused or wasted office supplies (stationery)?
- Have I misused work amenities such as a vehicle, travel allowance, and other benefits?
- Have I ever underperformed at work resulting in a loss to the company?
- Have I used the office computer/ internet for personal work without permission?
- Do I put my best effort in contributing to my company and its goals?
- Did I use my office hours to do my personal work (without permission)?
- Did I cheat on reporting my work hours?

Help the Poor, Generosity, Charity, and Exploiting the Poor

- Did I refuse help to anyone when it was within my power to help?
- Do I turn a blind eye to the cry of the poor and needy?
- Do I make the poor and needy to wait for my help?
- Do I make people wait, who come to me for help?
- Do I refuse to help others even when I have the money and resources?
- Do I see the people in need and not help them?

Reparation and Restitution

- Do I make a sincere effort to make restitution for the damages caused by my negligence and sinfulness?
- Have I failed to make restitution for the harm I caused to others?
- Do I make spiritual reparation (prayer and intercession) for people who were wounded by my sins?
- Do I pray for the victims of my sin and evil?

Stealing from Self

- Am I able to see myself as financially blessed?
- Are my prayers restricted to the desires and needs of this life?
- Am I content and happy with what I have?
- Is becoming rich the sole desire of my life?
- Do I have an obsession with wealth and power?
- Do I see wealth as power?
- Do I have an unhealthy desire to make money quickly without working for it?
- Do I trust wealth more than I trust God?

The Desire to Earn Money Quickly

- Am I addicted to gambling?
- Am I addicted or involved in excessive stock trading?
- Am I addicted to buying lottery tickets?

- Am I addicted to betting on games or races?

Illegal Ways of Earning Money

- Did I involve myself in any illegal business dealing?
- Did I buy or sell any banned substance?

Wisdom and Prudence in Spending and Saving

- Am I hasty in making financial decisions?
- Do I pray long enough before I take any significant or long-term financial decisions and investments?
- Do I use credit cards excessively and buy things on interest?
- Do I waste money?
- Am I lavish in my spending and lifestyle?
- Do I save money for the future?
- Have I been financially responsible?
- Do I waste or spend money unnecessarily?
- Do I misuse borrowed money?

Stinginess / Miserly Attitude

- Do I find it hard to part with my money even when it comes to meet my most basic need or to pay my bills?
- Do I always have to be compelled to give?
- Do I get angry at my family members if they spend for their basic needs?

- Am I obsessed with checking my bank balance/ bank account?

Gift Culture

- Do I feel hurt when I do not get any gift?
- Do I feel obligated to give gifts during Christmas and other occasions?
- Do I see giving and receiving of gifts as an expression of love?
- Do I measure the love of a person by the gift he or she gives?
- Do I waste too much money on gifts and holiday shopping?
- Do I flaunt my wealth (showoff culture)?

Stealing from Nature

- Do I waste food?
- Do I waste electricity or other energy that I use?
- Have I supported any scientific research that could potentially harm life or the natural world around us?
- Am I prompt in recycling?
- Am I careful in using natural resources, thereby causing minimum damage to nature?
- Did I destroy any natural resources for my selfish needs (deforestation)?
- Have I supported the use of nuclear, atomic, chemical, or biological weapons?

The Eighth Commandment

You shall not bear false witness against your neighbor

Misuse of Speech

False Witness

- Have I ever testified falsely in a court?
- Did I ever produce a false witness in a court to win a case?
- Did I ever, as a child, testify falsely against my sibling?
- Did I ever falsely testify at work resulting in penalties, suspension, or termination to any of my co-workers?
- Did I ever fail to take responsibility, or blame someone else for an accident I caused?

False Accusations

- Have I falsely accused anyone and not repented?
- Do I have the habit of accusing others of wrongdoing without verifying the facts?
- Have I falsely accused anyone out of hatred, envy, or jealousy?
- Did I ever falsely blame someone for a mistake or wrong that I committed?

- Did I file a case against anyone without verifying the facts?

Ridiculing / Mocking / Teasing / Making Fun

- Have I teased people based on their looks?
- Have I teased people for their race, community, nationality, color, etc.?
- Have I teased people for their weaknesses and failures?
- Have I bullied other kids when I was a kid?
- Do I imitate or make fun of my superiors behind their backs?
- Have I teased people for their accent or how they speak?
- Have I committed the sin of ragging?

Judging

- Do I entertain judgmental thoughts about anybody?
- Do I judge my superiors at work?
- Have I judged any religious person?
- Do I judge people for their work or performance?
- Am I a judgmental person?
- Have I been prejudiced toward others because of race, color, or religion?
- Have I judged anyone rashly based only on circumstantial evidence?

- Do I judge people for their sins/ failures/ weaknesses or actions?

Lying

- Do I remember any instance in my life where I lied and brought harm or disrepute to another person?
- Am I a habitual or chronic liar?
- Do I lie to my superiors/ teachers to cover up my mistakes?
- Do I keep secrets and lie to my spouse about it?
- Do I (teenage children) lie to my parents about my whereabouts?
- Do I lie in order not to hurt people's feelings?
- Do I (businesspeople) lie to my customers about the product I am selling?
- Do I lie about my age or my children's age to get some benefits?
- Do I lie when I must take a day off from work?
- Do I exaggerate facts?
- Have I failed to make reparation for a lie I told, or for harm done to a person's reputation?

Gossip/ Rumors/ Rash Judgement/ Calumny/ Detraction / Secrets

- Have I gossiped?
- Do I spread rumors?

- Do I actively and engagingly listen to gossip?
- Have I committed the sin of detraction (destroying a person's reputation by telling others about his faults for no good reason)?
- Have I committed the sin of calumny (telling lies about another person in order to destroy his reputation)?
- Have I committed the sin of libel (writing lies about another person in order to destroy a person's reputation)?
- Have I revealed or disclosed the faults, weaknesses, or failures of another person?
- Do I reveal the faults/ sins of my spouse or family members to a priest in the confessional?
- Do I reveal the faults of my loved ones or others to a third person, such as a counselor or coworker?
- Have I engagingly listened to the faults of other people shared by someone?
- Do I share the faults of celebrities/politicians that I receive on social media?
- Have I shared secrets that I am not allowed to share?
- Did I break any non-disclosure agreement?

Flattery (Failure to Correct)

- Do I have the habit of praising others with an ulterior motive?
- Do I flatter for a return favor?
- Do I exploit the weaknesses in people?

- Have I failed to correct and discipline people who are under my authority?

Self-Praise

- Do I seek and look for praise and compliments for what I do?
- Do I make myself available for praise, or do I praise myself?
- Do I boast?

Verbal Abuse / Verbal Attack / Verbal Assault)

- Have I cursed or wished harm to anyone?
- Have I wished the death of anyone?
- Have I prayed for somebody's harm or destruction?
- Have I criticized anyone publicly or behind their backs?
- Did I verbally abuse anyone?
- Do I condemn people with my words?
- Have I slandered or belittled others in my speech?

Foolish Talk / Crude Jokes / Profane Chatter / Bad and Obscene Language / Dirty Talk

- Do I use impure language while speaking?
- Do I overly engage in a foolish, idle, or unproductive talk?
- Did I engagingly listen to impure conversations?

- Do I watch or listen to shows that use bad, and profane language?

Imperfections in speech

- Do I always speak negatively about myself and other?
- Do I speak hastily without much thought?
- Do I speak carelessly?

The Ninth Commandment

You shall not covet your neighbor's wife

Purity of Vision

Looking with Lust

- Do I find it hard to control my eyes when I come across a beautiful person?
- Do I make a sincere effort to look away from a beautiful person?
- Do I look at people with lust?
- Do I secretly look at the private parts of people of the opposite sex?
- Do I look at people while they are displaying affection in public?
- Do I enjoy watching the beauty of any celebrity/ media person on television or the internet?
- Have I committed the sin of voyeurism (watching others when they are naked or engaged in sexual activity)?
- Do I sincerely avoid places where people are scantily clothed?

Purity of Heart

- Do I see people of the opposite sex as an object of lust?
- Am I fixated on the body parts of people?
- Do I mingle with people of the opposite sex with a secret sexual motive?
- Have I secretly desired or yearned for another person's spouse?
- Have I sexually fantasized about a person other than my spouse?
- Do I admire any movie or sports personality merely for their physical features?
- Did I take pleasure in impure thoughts or desires?
- Have I lustfully kissed or sexually touched someone?
- Did I take an interest in listening to music or jokes that are harmful to purity or read books that are immoral?
- Did I allow myself to be seduced?
- Have I dwelled on impure thoughts or fantasies for the purpose of arousal?

Modesty

- Have I seduced anyone using words or actions?
- Do I have the habit of wearing indecent, skimpy, and revealing clothes (immodest dressing)?
- Do I flirt with the opposite sex, thereby tempting them and causing them to fall into sin?

The Tenth Commandment

You shall not covet your neighbor's goods

Intentions of the Heart

- What is the driving force behind all my actions?
- Is making money and becoming rich, the sole purpose of my life?
- Have I hurt or harmed anybody because of my greed or covetousness?
- Do I promptly return goods that I borrow from others?
- Do I have a passion for riches and a rich lifestyle?
- Am I selfish?
- Am I self-centered?
- Do I do all things for my own self-glory?
- Do I use (misuse or exploit) people for my personal and selfish gain?

The Capital Sins

(Seven Deadly Sins / Cardinal Sins)

Pride

- Did I look down (haughtiness) on anyone?
- Am I arrogant, or did I show arrogance?
- Did I boast, or am I a boastful person?
- Am I prideful of my possessions?
- Do I feel superior to others because of my abilities?
- Do I feel superior to others because of my accomplishments?
- Do I take pride in my looks?
- Do I see my race/ creed and culture/ family tradition/ community/ color to be superior to others?
- Do I have the habit of justifying myself (Self- Justification)?
- Am I open to corrections and able to submit to the one who is correcting me for my good?
- Am I always finding fault with others?
- Am I slow to find my own faults?

- Am I always critical of other people?
- Do I have the habit of pretending before others, trying to portray what I am not?
- Do I find it hard to seek help when I need it?
- Am I defensive when people try to correct me?
- Do I get irritated when I am contradicted?
- Am I hungry for praise and attention?
- Do I have a high opinion about myself?
- Do I look down upon others (haughty eyes)?
- Do I easily get angry when I do not get my way (a sign of wounded pride)?
- Do I find it hard to work under authority or take orders?
- Do I find it hard to forgive people (it requires humility to forgive)?
- Do I feel offended if I am not acknowledged or thanked?
- Do I get repeated judgmental thoughts resulting in gossip?
- Do I easily get hurt by words and insults of people?
- Do I find it hard to serve others because I feel I am superior to them ?
- Do I find it hard to seek forgiveness from others?
- Do I have the mentality that I deserve everything I have and more?
- Do I act humble only to receive praise from others?

- Do I practice false humility?
- Do I find it hard to be thankful to others for their help and support?
- Do I find it hard to work as a team?
- Do I find it hard to submit before God? (A humble person will have no difficulty kneeling, raising his hands, prostrating during prayer)
- Do I have a show-off attitude?
- Am I arrogant toward people under me?
- Do I have a self-centered and selfish attitude, always thinking and talking about myself?
- Do I yield to other people's ideas and plans?
- Do I listen to people, and am I an approachable person?
- Do I put myself first in everything I do?
- Do I reject authority at home, work, and Church?
- Am I frustrated about my weaknesses?
- Do I boast about myself?

Spiritual Pride

- Am I angry at people who are not interested in spiritual matters?
- Do I feel good about myself after accomplishing the daily spiritual activities?

- Do I get judgmental thoughts toward the Church and the religious?
- Do I judge and gossip about priests/ religious who are not serious about their ministry or vocation?
- Do I have hatred/hostility toward people outside the Church or other religions?
- Do I try to please God with my spiritual activities, thereby undermining his love and mercy?
- Am I angry and disappointed with myself over failure to accomplish spiritual goals?
- Do I find joy when someone compliments my dedication to God?

Avarice or Greed

- Is getting rich, the primary goal in my life?
- Do I have a history of not paying back my creditors?
- Am I overworking to earn more money?
- Does it hurt me when I must give money to others?
- Do I always make an excuse not to tithe?
- Do I have an unhealthy attachment to material possessions?
- Am I always into watching money related television shows or reading money-related magazines and books?
- Am I involved in, or operating more businesses than what I can handle?

- Is money the driving force behind all my decisions and activities?
- Do I live in moderation?
- Do I have a consumer mentality?

Envy

- Have I ever been saddened by the success and achievements of my spouse?
- Have I ever been saddened or felt angry over the achievements or successes of my friends and peers?
- Have I ever been saddened by the news of my friends or family member who is having a child before me or is getting married before me?
- Have I been saddened by the financial growth of others (family and friends)?
- Do I overwork or stress myself to have or afford what others have?
- Am I genuinely happy over other's successes?
- Do I show compassion and console people when they experience a loss?
- Do I, because of my envy, put undue pressure on my children concerning their education and performance?
- Am I unhappy about my poverty or my financial condition?
- Is my attitude of hard work borne out of envy?
- Did I envy the blessings received by others?

Wrath or Anger

- Did I get angry over things I cannot control?
- Did I get angry unjustly?
- Did I hurt anyone physically in a state of anger?
- Did I hurt anyone emotionally in a state of anger?
- Did I block communication because of anger?
- Did I block love and fellowship because of my anger?
- Did I yield to uncontrolled anger (anger without restraint)?
- Did I avoid anyone due to my anger and resentment?
- Did I seek revenge as a result of my anger?
- Did I destroy public or personal property in a state of anger?

Lust

- Am I always tempted to look at beautiful people?
- Do I always favor or side with good looking people?
- Did I pervert justice because of my lust?
- Have I engaged in sexual fantasies?
- Am I a worldly person?
- Am I living a life solely for amusement and pleasure?
- Am I living by the desires of my flesh and depriving the needs of the soul?

Gluttony

- Is there an unhealthy craving for delicious or exotic food in me?
- Am I always seeking a variety of food items or dishes?
- Does my eating habit conflict with my spiritual life and work?
- Do I fast regularly (if I am healthy)?
- Do I easily get irritated if the food is not tasty or if I do not get food on time?
- Do I eat hastily?
- Am I always thinking about food?
- Am I always eating?
- Am I fussy about a certain kind of food?
- Am I meticulous about eating only a particular cuisine?
- Does my love for food in any way affect my job and responsibilities?
- Do I always overeat (eating in excess)?

Sloth

Spiritual Sloth

- Do I find it hard to make sacrifices for the Lord?
- Am I happy with my spiritual growth, or is it stagnant?

- Do I sincerely and joyfully use the God-given gifts for the kingdom?
- Do I find spiritual activities boring and tiring?
- Do I always look at the clock when I pray?
- Do I always feel sleepy and tired during prayer time?
- Do I show aversion to spiritual matters?

Work and Responsibilities

- Am I always looking for quick ways to make money without any desire to work?
- Am I losing interest or meaning to life?
- Do I see work as a burden?
- Do I make false excuses to avoid work (indolence)?
- Do I see work as solely a means to earn money?
- Do I procrastinate?
- Am I thankful to God for work?
- Does my sleep habits hinder my work, responsibilities, and prayer life?
- Is money the only driving force for all the work I do?
- Do I do all my work to the best of my ability?
- Do I hate or show indifference toward work?
- Am I always told to work or fulfill my responsibilities?
- Do I spend my time in idleness?
- Do I spend a lot of time entertaining myself?

The Precepts of the Church

Whoever listens to you listens to me, and whoever rejects you rejects me, and whoever rejects me rejects the one who sent me. (Luk 10:16)

The precepts are general rules of the Catholic Church meant to guarantee the basic or necessary minimum one must fulfill in spiritual matters. In addition to the Ten Commandments, it is a good practice to regularly examine our conscience based on the precepts of the church to see if we are following the fundamental laws. The precepts were covered in detail within the commandments in this book; therefore, no further explanation is given here.

A word of caution to the reader; if we base our life on the bare minimum, little of what is left will be taken away from us. We should strive to excel and reach perfection in our faith life. Our love for God is not genuine if we try to fulfill only the minimum requirements of the church.

As you therefore have received Christ Jesus the Lord, continue to live your lives in him, rooted and built up in him and established in the faith, just as you were taught. (Col 2:6-7)

Below are the five precepts of the Church.

The First Precept

You shall attend Mass on Sundays and holy days of obligation and rest from work.

The Second Precept

You shall confess your sins at least once a year.

The Third Precept

You shall receive Jesus in the Eucharist at least during the Easter season.

The Fourth Precept

You shall observe the Church's prescribed days of fasting and abstinence.

The Fifth Precept

You shall assist to provide for the material needs of the Church.

Conclusion

A Catholic is foremost expected to be faithful and committed to his parish. People come together to form a parish. Without the people of God, there will be no parish. Praying with the parish and for the parish is the duty of every parishioner. A parish needs intercession and prayer support to operate. It is important that we understand and play our role in our parish and the Mother Church. The next chapter looks at another important teaching, which summarizes all that this book has covered so far.

The Great Commandment

Just as I have loved you, you also should love one another. (Jn 13:34)

The Commandment of Love

All the Old Testament commandments can be summarized to two commandments in the New Testament; love for God and love for neighbor. The two commandments can be combined into one, which is the only commandment to obey and follow. Love is the only commandment and the greatest. He who loves has fulfilled the law. Sin is the absence of love, and to love is what we owe to our God and neighbor.

Owe no one anything, except to love one another; for the one who loves another has fulfilled the law. (Rom 13:8)

Love for God

God is love, and he created everything in love, for love, and to love. He created us in love and filled us with his love. Original sin wounded our capacity and ability to love. Our love is wounded because of our iniquities. It is not steadfast, abundant, and free-flowing. It is selfish and centered toward self. As a result, it takes an effort to love. We are fully capable of loving, and it is not impossible for us. Jesus modeled love for us. Therefore, meditating on the gospels and the life of Jesus will teach us to love like him. All things must be done with love, including our spiritual activities. To love God with all our heart, mind, body, soul, and spirit is the first commandment.

To love him with all the heart, and with all the understanding, and with all the strength,' and 'to love one's neighbor as oneself,' – this is much more important than all whole burnt offerings and sacrifices." (Mrk 12:33)

Jesus combined the love for God and love for our neighbor as one commandment making it inseparable. Therefore, our love for God is demonstrated in our ability to love our neighbor, and the love of neighbor can be fulfilled only if we deeply love God.

Those who say, "I love God," and hate their brothers or sisters, are liars; for those who do not love a brother or sister whom they have seen, cannot love God whom they have not seen. (1 Jn 4:20)

True love casts out all sin and evil. We cannot do evil to somebody we truly love. Love by itself has the power to destroy all evil. God is love, and those who abide in love abide in God, and God abides in them. Jesus, through his unconditional love for the father and all humanity, won the victory over evil and death.

- Do I love God with all my heart, mind, body, soul, spirit, and strength?
- Do I love God, above all else?
- Do all my spiritual activities proceed with love and centered on love?
- Is God my first love?

Love for Neighbor

Do I love my neighbor the way I want to be loved by others? By far, this is the easiest commandment to explain, but the hardest to follow. Jesus used the words "love your neighbor as yourself," leaving us a lot to work on. How do I want to be loved? I don't want to be hurt by anybody. Therefore I have no right to hurt anybody either. If I want others to be compassionate and forgiving toward me, I should also be returning that treatment to others. What we look for in people, they look in us for those qualities. We should be willing to do to others as we would want them to do for us.

The commandments, "You shall not commit adultery; You shall not murder; You shall not steal; You shall not covet"; and any other commandment, are summed up in this word, "Love your neighbor as yourself. (Rom 13:9)

- Do I love others the way I want to be loved?
- Am I a religious person with no love for my neighbor?
- Do I do all things in love?
- Do I love everyone unconditionally?
- Do I love everyone with God's love?
- Do I love and pray for those who persecute me?

Quick Examination of Conscience for Confession

- Have I denied the existence of God?
- Have I deliberately missed my daily prayer or scripture reading?
- Have I treated people or anything of this world as more important than God?
- Have I spoken against the Catholic teachings on the Blessed Mother, saints, and angels? Have I shown irreverence to any heavenly beings?
- Have I deliberately denied any of the Church's teachings?
- Have I practiced any non-Catholic religious teachings?
- Have I practiced any superstitions?
- Have I practiced any occult activities?
- Have I shown irreverence to consecrated people, things, places, and times?
- Have I mocked, insulted, blasphemed the name of God?
- Have I abused the sacraments in any way?
- Have I shown irreverence to the Holy Spirit by deliberately showing unbelief toward the gifts and Charisms?
- Have I complained and grumbled about my problems (sin of ingratitude)?
- Have I missed Mass on Sunday since my last confession?
- Have I received communion irreverently?
- Have I been disobedient or disrespectful to my parents?
- Have I mistreated my spouse or my children?

- Have I committed abortion or aided in abortion?
- Have I killed anyone?
- Have I deliberately entertained suicidal thoughts or considered suicide?
- Do I have hatred, bitterness, or resentment toward anyone?
- Have I abused my body in anyway (lack of rest, harmful sports, overeating, lack of sleep, etc)?
- Have I abused any substance (Tobacco, drugs, alcohol)?
- Have I committed adultery?
- Have I committed fornication?
- Have I committed acts of homosexuality?
- Have I committed the sin of masturbation?
- Have I watched pornography?
- Have I committed the sin of prostitution?
- Have I denied my spouse his or her conjugal rights?
- Have I used artificial birth control methods?
- Have I taken or offered bribe?
- Have I stolen anything?
- Have I gambled excessively?
- Have I lied?
- Have I slandered, gossiped, or spread rumors?
- Have I falsely accused anyone?
- Have I judged anyone?
- Have I looked at women with lust?
- Have I entertained or taken pleasure in impure thoughts?

How to Confess

- Begin your confession with the sign of the cross (In the name of the Father, and the Son, and the Holy Spirit, Amen)
- Bless me, Father, for I have sinned. My last confession was______ (days/weeks/months/years) ago.
- List out your sins. Confess all the sins and how many times you committed them.
- Conclude by saying, "I am sorry for these sins and the sins I fail to remember."
- Wait for the priest's advice. Listen carefully to what the priest has to say. Most priests encourage the sinner by drawing them out of guilt and taking them to the love and mercy of God. They may also suggest or give some practical advice to overcome certain sins.

Act of Contrition

At this time, the priest will ask the penitent to recite the act of contrition. Some priests may ask the repentant to say this prayer along with the penance, outside the confessional. This prayer is essential and must be recited at some point, either in the confessional or when saying the penance, because it opens our heart to God. It is our way of telling God that we have hurt and wounded him and would like to return to him. There is more than one form of this prayer. One may choose whichever kind one is comfortable praying. The prayer goes like this,

O my God, I am heartily sorry for having offended Thee, and I detest all my sins because of Thy just punishments, but most of all because they

offend Thee, my God, who art all-good and deserving of all my love. I firmly resolve, with the help of Thy grace, to sin no more and to avoid the near occasions of sin.

Penance

Followed by the act of contrition, the priest will give a penance to the penitent. It is an exercise for the spiritual good of the repentant. Penance can be in the form of a prayer, namely, the Our Father, the Hail Mary, or any prayer that the priest may recommend offering it for the victim of sin if there is any. Some priests recommend reading a chapter of the Psalms or other books in the Bible. Others may instruct the penitent to spend some quiet time in front of the Blessed Sacrament. It is up to the priest at the confessional.

Absolution and Final Blessing

Finally, the priest will recite the prayer of absolution. To absolve is to free someone from guilt or blame or sin. At this time, the penitent listens carefully to the words of the priest. The formula is universal and goes like this.

God, the Father of mercies,
through the death and the resurrection of his Son
has reconciled the world to himself
and sent the Holy Spirit among us
for the forgiveness of sins;
through the ministry of the Church
may God give you pardon and peace,
and I absolve you from your sins in the name of the Father, and of the Son and of the Holy Spirit.

Thank the priest and leave the confessional. Find a quiet corner in the church. If the Blessed Sacrament is exposed, you may sit before the Lord or sit where the tabernacle is located. Do the penance with all sincerity.

Made in the USA
Monee, IL
02 February 2024

52821416R00057